RELATIONSHIP GOAL

V K MORPHEUS

Copyright © V K Morpheus
All Rights Reserved.

ISBN 979-888606929-7

This book has been published with all efforts taken to make the material error-free after the consent of the author. However, the author and the publisher do not assume and hereby disclaim any liability to any party for any loss, damage, or disruption caused by errors or omissions, whether such errors or omissions result from negligence, accident, or any other cause.

While every effort has been made to avoid any mistake or omission, this publication is being sold on the condition and understanding that neither the author nor the publishers or printers would be liable in any manner to any person by reason of any mistake or omission in this publication or for any action taken or omitted to be taken or advice rendered or accepted on the basis of this work. For any defect in printing or binding the publishers will be liable only to replace the defective copy by another copy of this work then available.

TO

MY KOCHU

THIS BOOK IS

AFFECTIONATELY DEDICATED

Contents

Foreword

The book featured about different kind of relationship and tips to makes valuable one in future.

Preface

Each relationship will have its promising and less promising times. All through your relationship, you are probably going to run into various obstacles.

It isn't these knocks themselves that will represent the moment of truth a relationship; it is the way you can deal with them all together. A solid relationship is one where the two players are prepared to explore the uneven way and work together to take care of issues.

Acknowledgements

My deepest thanks to my close and supportive circle of friends. ... Lastly, very special thanks to my family, who have endured the writing of the book.

Prologue

Relationships like they say are most certainly made in paradise anyway it's anything but a ruddy undertaking. It is a rollercoaster ride where you will have a few squabbles, contentions and battles; there will be minutes when you need to kill your significant other for being so irritating.

Husband and Wife

Marriage is one of the most perfect foundation and bond divided among two individuals. There is a justification for why individuals take promises and it is your obligation to ensure you adhere to every last one of them. Relationships like they say are most certainly made in paradise anyway it's anything but a ruddy undertaking. It is a rollercoaster ride where you will have a few squabbles, contentions and battles; there will be minutes when you need to kill your significant other for being so irritating. In this, what ammeters the most is the way that you both outperform all of this nevertheless loves each other like you have done 100% of the time. You want to stick through all of this, clasping hands.

A smidgen of understanding, a great deal of tolerance and a few cognizant endeavors are all you really want to keep a decent connection with your significant other. Also after so long or for the recently married lady, on the off chance that you actually are don't know about the numerous ways on the most proficient method to keep a decent connection with your better half, then, at that point, this is the place where you ought to be. We will assist you for certain successful and idiot proof tips.

Tips for wife

1. Be decent audience

On the off chance that your significant other gets back home following a tiring day at work and you notice he is anxious, put him down and request that he share his day with you. Try not to begin your own pressures and protests since that will just aggravate him.

Be a decent audience and assist him with easing up.

2. Invest great energy with your significant other

This s something vital to do that most couples frequently wind up overlooking. You really want to guarantee that you invest quality energy with your significant other. Regardless of how bustling you and occurs, you both should get some down time for yourselves. Converse with one another, go out on dates and simply do all two or three things.

3. Genuineness ought to be kept up with

Regardless at all, you really want to guarantee that there is genuineness. Extends don't lie about anything in light of the fact that once you lie; you will be enticed to do it more regularly. We are certain your significant other will see the value in your genuineness.

4. Some of the time let go

There will be times when your better half battles with you in any event, when it isn't your shortcoming. It is OK for the sake of adoration to give up off such thing s on occasion. Simply consent to what he says and continue on. Anyway don't do this generally in case he could begin underestimating you.

5. Never speak more loudly when irate

Like we said before, battles and fights are ordinary in each relationship. Anyway never holler at your significant other or speak more loudly. This could hurt his male inner self and things can deteriorate before you understand. In the event that you have an issue, get it to his notification an inconspicuous yet harsh way.

6. Revive the lost flash and sentiment

the main thing to do is keep your connection alive and dynamic. As years pass, a few couples simply become acclimated to the every day schedule and do nothing unique. So revive the sentiment, go on dates, shock him, think of him love notes and cook dinners, etc.

Follow these straightforward sort yet vital hints and you can share a solid, blissful and heartfelt wedded existence with your better half.

Tips for husband

1. Love

A man's most prominent need is to be regarded, and a lady's most noteworthy need is to be cherished. Exhibiting your adoration doesn't have to be a sumptuous illicit relationship, yet it should be a vital piece of everyday life. Love to a lady is seldom pretty much sex. From the manner in which you address her in private and public, to whether or not you add to overseeing errands at home, to the time you spend together on ends of the week - each and every demonstration you truly do can say a lot to your significant other. There will, obviously, be days when your better half appears to be repulsive, potentially after cruel words have been traded or an apparently irrational solicitation made, yet recall that nobody is awesome. Recollect your marriage pledges, to adore and value "for better in negative ways".

2. Know her main avenue for affection

We all give and get love in various ways, and perhaps the best gift you can give towards your marriage is to get yourself and your companion's ways to express affection. As per therapist Gary Chapman, the five fundamental ways to express affection are Words of Affirmation, Quality Time, Gifts, Acts of Service and Physical Touch.

3. Treat her with tenderness and regard _ Indeed, even the most autonomous, decisive lady needs an accomplice who will treat her with tenderness and regard. Not out of dread of bringing about her fury, nor out of a feeling of male predominance that considers her powerless and insufficient, however out of a real craving to lead the marriage as a visual demonstration and honor his significant other.

4. Listen well

Most men are regular issue solvers and float towards tracking down the answer for any issue that introduces itself, including your better half's. Then again, most ladies are not as keen on tackling their concerns as they are in tracking down somebody to come close by them in the excursion. Your significant other needs your sympathy, not your ideas. She needs you to save your paper to pay attention to her portion, not really for you to get over her concerns as "unimportant". Folks, figure out how to listen well to your companion first and examine choices later.

5. Set aside a few minutes for sentiment

Whenever a marriage starts, it doesn't imply that your dating days are finished. Frequently, the day by day daily practice of regular day to day existence can crush out the sparkles of sentiment that were such a lot of a piece of your romance and it will require exertion from the two players to keep the fire alive. Sentiment starts at home - from the humblest things, such as making her morning meal in bed, or astonishing her with a bundle of her cherished sprouts. Plan one-on-one unique dates on commemorations and birthday celebrations and irregular days in the middle. Make time to share your fantasies,

plan your next occasion, talk about your feelings of dread,
or even investigate another leisure activity together.

Love versus " Arranged Marriages"

Marriage is a common agreement between a man and a lady. Marriage is a lawful agreement between two people that prompts family relationship. These days, one can find out about affection relationships and organized relationships, which have a few distinctions between them.

Dissimilar to organized relationships, love relationships are more normal in the Western World. Indeed, what precisely is an organized marriage and love marriage? An organized marriage is a marriage which is organized by people other than the individuals who are getting hitched. Then again, an affection marriage is a marriage which is organized by the actual accomplices.

In organized relationships, the couples should the assent of their folks. Then again, in a large portion of the affection Relationships, the accomplices won't require the assent of the guardians, or seniors.

Not at all like love relationships, organized relationships are more steady. Divorces are seen less in organized relationships, and there is an extraordinary family bond.

In organized relationships, the guardians will be completely exploring the foundation of the lady of the hour and the lucky man.

They will be investigating each angle, similar to riches, medical issue and propensities. In adoration relationships, the couples are not stressed over any foundation examinations. It is simply love that runs in their blood.

While discussing love, love must be created in an organized marriage, as they will just know one another better after the wedlock, yet in an affection marriage, the couples have forever been enamored, and there is no compelling reason to foster it.

In organized relationships, the couples will be unable to see each other quite well, and furthermore not have a clue about the preferences of one another.

Something else that is seen in organized relationships is that men are more prevailing all of the time than the ladies. In adoration marriage, the couples stretch out beyond the wedlock. In such relationships, nobody is by all accounts predominant individual over the other.

Synopsis:

1. An organized marriage is a marriage that is organized by people other than the two who are getting hitched. Then again, an affection marriage is a marriage which is organized by the actual accomplices.

2. Dissimilar to adore relationships, organized relationships are more steady.

3. In an organized marriage, the couples should get the assent of their folks. Then again, in the majority of affection relationships, the accomplices won't require the assent of the guardians, or older folks.

4. In organized relationships, men are more predominant all of the time than ladies.

Breakup

The principal thing to do is to comprehend that separations are hard. Be thoughtful to yourself what you're feeling is absolutely regular. "It's essential to comprehend that first and foremost, your body will be in a condition of shock.

What Next?

1. Keep Yourself Busy

You will be enticed to connect with your ex - so make an arrangement to limit that allurement by zeroing in on yourself. "You can keep yourself occupied for the initial fourteen days," Chan says. "Get your vibe great synthetics from investing energy with companions, local area, and taking care of oneself. Get your endorphins moving by working out (hello, this is an extraordinary-Opportunity to evaluate that new dance class you've been thinking about)."

2. Contact Others For Support

You will be feeling the loss of your ex, yet rather than messaging them, connect with others. This can be your companions, your family, a specialist - as long as it isn't your ex. "Persuade a companion to be your responsibility accomplice, since discipline isn't your companion during the phase of recuperation," Chan recommends.

3.Try not to Check Their Social Media

In spite of the fact that it will be enticing to Insta-tail your ex, give your all to oppose that enticement. Chan prompts, "Before you actually look at his Instagram, pause and ask, 'Am I being thoughtful to myself at the present Time?' You know the response. Supplant the desire with one more conduct that drives you to be available. This might mean you call a companion, go for a run, or compose a letter of appreciation to somebody you love. The initial not many times you redirect your conduct it will feel devised and very testing, yet the more you work on supplanting the behaving destructively encourage with a sound practice, the simpler it becomes."

4. Do a Digital Detox

Alongside trying not to check your ex's socials, Chan recommends eliminating their presence from your telephone. Indeed, that implies unfriending or obstructing your ex via online media. Assuming you're hesitant to do this, remember that you can constantly re-companion them later, when the tragedy isn't really new. "Erase old messages, photographs, unfollow their records, and, surprisingly, better, enjoy some time off from web-based media out and out," Chan says. "Block their number assuming that you need to, so you don't fixate on them not reaching you."

5. Change Up Your Physical Space _ After a separation, switching around your actual space can help you intellectually re-set. Assuming you live respectively, move out when you're ready to. In the event that you don't live respectively - or regardless of whether you - change up your space. This can be just about as basic as washing your bed covers and taking care of that outlined photograph of you two, or it very well may be a complete overhaul of your space.

"The more you can diminish your openness to recollections of your ex, the more you limit your possibilities of backslide," Chan says. "Move around your furnishings, improve on the things in your home and allegorically account for the new to come in."

6.Whatever You Do, Don't Have Breakup Sex

You will need to have separation sex - yet don't, Chan says. While it's simply normal to need to, in the event that you really do have separation sex, "you are laying out a passionate bond whether or not you like it. So assuming that you're attempting to move past somebody, in a real sense, don't get on top of them! Sex with the ex is restricting those bonds to break, keeping you more joined."

7. Plan Something Fun - Without Your Ex

Making new recollections without your ex can assist you with starting to continue on. "Book a taking care of oneself occasion so you have something to anticipate,"

Chan says. "Pick something sound like a yoga retreat, or Renew Breakup Bootcamp."

8. Think about Your Relationship

After the prompt torment has passed, think back on your relationship and reflect. "At times a separation is the purge required when you want to divert your life," Chan says. "Separations are an extraordinary chance to go internal, to assess what examples are there for you to develop, to advance, to be more cognizant. Torment is an amazing inspiration change. Utilize the aggravation as fuel to your fire to make the life and love you want."

Friendship Goal

1. Be genuine

Individuals are switched off by the people who are continually attempting to be somebody else. We are generally agreeable around other people who are happy with just being themselves. So act naturally.

Despite the fact that you're flawed, the manner in which you handle your assets and deficiencies with lowliness and certainty will allow others to be genuine and loose with you, also. Genuine companions are loose around one another.

2. Be straightforward

Stay true to your obligations and do what you say you will do. Be dependable. No one needs to be companions with somebody who lies. Furthermore lies generally have an approach to coming to the light. Additionally, companions will say reality to each other, in any event, when it's hard. The savvies man in the Bible, King Solomon, said: Faithful are the injuries of a companion, yet the kisses of a foe are underhanded. Shannon became involved with a dietary problem until her companion got down on her: I was dependent on being thin and looking totally awesome. I never truly comprehended how I was really treating myself until an old buddy of mine conversed with me regarding it.

3. Check out the subtleties of your companion's life by being a decent audience

Try not to stare at the TV or text while your companion is offering something to you. Most times individuals need more than solid counsel, they need somebody to stand by listening to them as they talk through their sentiments. Ask them what's happening in their life and how they feel. Mari remarked: Kyler is my closest companion since he tunes in. Regardless is going on he is really intrigued by how I am.

He generally has me covered and would drop everything assuming that I wanted him.

4. Set aside a few minutes for your companion

Time is probably the best gift we have. Whenever we share additional time with a companion, we are rewarding them that gift. No fellowship can grow for the time being.

It requires some investment. A genuine companion will take that time.

5. Stay discreet

Substantiate yourself to be a reliable individual who will watch their insider facts with your life. A decent method for demonstrating you are dependable is to be allowed to impart your very own portion insider facts to your companion. Ruler Solomon likewise said: Friends come and companions go- However a genuine companion sticks by you like family. Is it true or not that you will be a companion like that?

6. Energize your companion

Everybody needs consolation. Track down explicit ways of empowering your companion. Indeed, even in the profundities of their battles, demonstrate them what you see to be extraordinary with regards to them and get them when they are discouraged or feel like life is squeezing in on them from all sides.

7. Be faithful to your companion

This is genuine acknowledgment, in any event, when your companion commits an error or truly messes up. Be there when they are encountering their most elevated highs and their least lows. Chuckle with them, cry with them, don't simply discuss continuously being there. Demonstrate it in your regular daily existence! Delaney kept in touch with me and said: I have incredible companions who are dependably there for myself and consistently know how to fulfill me.

8. Work through struggle

Each relationship will hit a hindrance at some time. Show your companion you will deal with the troublesome seasons of errors and . Some of the time companionships develop further through troublesome times. Try not to abandon your companion since you are experiencing issues.

9. Look out for your companion

Whenever you see your companion getting into a risky circumstance whether it's with medications or liquor, or perhaps a disastrous relationship, be striking to the point of stepping in and safeguarding your companion from the damage you see coming their direction.

Sibling relationships

Regardless of how unique your children are from each other, kin bonds are significant. As a parent, there are a few things you can do to cultivate the connections between your children, which will ideally be deep rooted.

1. Try not to Compare Your Kids

Most importantly, make an effort not to make statements like, "For what reason would you be able to tune in as well as your sibling does?" or "Your sister doesn't nitpick me." Comparing your kids to one another is a certain fire method for stirring up the flames of kin contention and fabricate disdain.

2.Figure Out What's Behind Sibling Conflicts

Do your children will quite often quarrel when one is attempting to stand out? Could it be said that they are seeking your time and consideration? Do they battle more when they are worn out or exhausted?

When you see an example that could clarify this conduct, attempt to resolve those issues to limit kin quarrels. For example, you can have a go at investing one-on-one energy with every youngster or attempt to assist your kid With viewing as better, non-alienating ways of standing out enough to be noticed.

3. Have Them Team Up for Chores One of the manners in which organizations assemble a feeling of collaboration and participation among their staff is by having representatives participate in activities and exercises that empower cooperating. Guardians can accomplish something almost identical with their kids, either by having children cooperate on an undertaking or help each other with tasks.

Concoct an undertaking, like composition an extra room or wiping out the carport, and have children cooperate to make it happen. You can likewise have children take on tasks that are best for their age and capacities, for example, clearing or getting ready supper and have them race against the adults in the house to see who finishes their errands quicker.

Making the messes with one group and the adults another can urge children to cooperate toward a shared objective beating their folks.

4. Assemble Their Listening Skills

The capacity to truly pay attention to what somebody is talking about is a significant expertise for youngsters to create, and one that assists them with figuring out how to understand others and see things according to another person's perspective. Make it a highlight have kin tune in and make a decent attempt to see each other's perspectives and considerations.

Show the Importance of Respect

Listening is one method for recognizing one another, and regard is vital for building great connections, regardless of whether it's between companions, accomplices, or kin. Remind kids that they Should treat others the manner in which they need to be dealt with, with thoughtfulness and worry for their feelings.Respect can incorporate conversing With one another utilizing a decent or if nothing else not terrible manner of speaking, in any event, while deviating; not putting down a kin's viewpoints; and being aware of another person's space and effects (not going into a kin's room without consent or contacting their things, for example).

5. Tell Them The best way to Respectfully Skills

Individuals who love each other can differ some of the time - that is only an unavoidable truth. In any case, it's the manner by which we handle those conflicts that matter. Show your kids that they may not consistently agree things, yet that they should not call each other names, let contentions influence their positive associations, and in particular, participate in actual battling.

6. Underline Family Bonding

Disclose to your kids and remind them intermittently that family, and particularly kin, can be the sort of enduring adoration and backing that can only with significant effort be coordinated.

Remind your youngsters that while they may regularly incline toward the organization of companions over a sibling or sister now, they will turn out to be more essential to one another as they grow up.

While they may not totally comprehend the significance of kin connections yet, this is a message that merits rehashing, and one that they will ultimately develop to acknowledge as they age.

7. Set aside a few minutes for Fun

Families who have some good times together will be more averse to have struggle. Attempt to pick games and exercises that can be delighted in by the entire family, like riding bicycles or watching an extraordinary new film for Bonds.

Brother-sister relationship according to me is the most unconditional and attached relationship. We all know that the opposite genders get along well as "opposites attract". Imagine having an opposite gender sibling, who'll be your best friend and family throughout your life. You're really blessed.

8.Teach Siblings to Appreciate Each Other's Differences

Do you have one kid who loves to sit and peruse discreetly and another who prefers nothing better compared to clearly games and consistent exercises? Whenever youngsters have totally different interests and dispositions, clashes can normally happen.

The significant thing is to show kids how to regard those distinctions, and how to watch out for what's truly significant: Loving one another. To pick a family action that consolidates a ton of activity while another youngster needs to accomplish something peaceful and serene, you could set up a framework where they can cooperate to arrange for how to alternate or observe other normal interests that can be a good time for the two kin.

Parent - Child

1. Show Your Love

Human touch and adoring friendship is required at each phase of our lives for solid enthusiastic and neurobiological turn of events. Your youngster actually must get delicate, cherishing contact (i.e., embraces) from you a few times over the course of the day. Treat each communication as a chance to associate with your youngster. Welcome them with warm articulations, give eye to eye connection, grin, and support fair communication.

2. Say "I love you" frequently

It is generally expected suggested that we love our youngsters, however make certain to let them know consistently, regardless age they are. In any event- when your kid is being troublesome or accomplishes something you don't like; this can be a great chance to advise them that you love them genuinely.

A straightforward "I love you" can significantly affect your drawn out relationship with your youngster.

3. Set limits, rules, and results

Kids need design and direction as they develop and find out regarding their general surroundings. Converse with your youngsters concerning what you expect of them and ensure they comprehend. At the point when rules are broken, try to have age-suitable outcomes set up and be steady with them.

4. Listen and identify

Association begins with tuning in.

Recognize your youngster's sentiments, show them you comprehend, and console them that you are there to assist with anything they need. Attempt to see things according to your kid's point of view.

By tuning in and identifying with your youngster, you will start to cultivate common regard.

5. Play Together

Play is so critical to a kid's turn of events. It is the instrument through which youngsters foster language abilities, express feelings, cultivate innovativeness, and find out regarding interactive abilities. Furthermore, it is a great way for you to reinforce your relationship with your kid. It doesn't make any difference what you play. The key is to simply partake in one another and focus on actually focusing on your kid.

6. Be accessible and interruption free

Saving only 10 minutes per day to converse with to your kid, without interruptions, can have a major effect in laying out great correspondence propensities.

Switch off the TV, set aside your electronic gadgets, and get to know each other. Your youngster has to realize that you accept they are fundamentally important in your life regardless of the numerous interruptions and stressors that come your direction.

7. Eat suppers together

Eating all together can regularly prompt extraordinary discussion and holding time with your youngster. Urge everybody to take care of their telephones or different gadgets and basically appreciate each other's conversation. Supper time is additionally an extraordinary chance for you to show your youngsters the significance of a solid and adjusted diet, which likewise impacts there in general psychological wellness.

8. Make parent-kid ceremonies

In the event that you have more than one kid, attempt to try investing individual energy with every one of them. Quality, one-on-one time with your youngster can fortify the parent-kid bond, develops your kid's confidence, and tells them that they are exceptional and esteemed.

A few guardians plan for extraordinary "date evenings" with their youngsters to make that one-on-a single an open door (regardless of whether it's a stroll around the area, an outing to the jungle gym, or simply a film at home - it's essential to praise every kid exclusively).

Thank You

It's some ideas about make good relationship so, read and set your own views and insight.

Dear Reader, Thank You!

9 798886 069297